This book belongs to

....

When dinosaurs ruled

by Lucy Waterhouse

Can you find
a snail on
every page?

make
believe
ideas

Get the most from this reader

• •

Before reading:

● Look at the pictures and discuss
   them together. Ask questions such as,
   "What do you think these dinosaurs ate?"

● Relate the topic to your child's
   world. For example, say:
   "What other animals do we
   know with long necks?"

● Familiarise your child with book
   vocabulary by using terms such as
   word, *letter*, *title*, *author* and *text*.

• •

During reading:

● Prompt your child to sound out unknown words.
   Draw attention to neglected middle or end sounds.

● Encourage your child to use the pictures as
   clues to unknown words.

● Occasionally ask what might happen next,
   and then check together as you read on.

- Monitor your child's understanding. Repeated readings can improve fluency and comprehension.

- Keep reading sessions short and enjoyable. Stop if your child becomes tired or frustrated.

• •

After reading:

- Discuss the book. Encourage your child to form opinions with questions such as, "What did you like best about this book?"

- Help your child work through the fun activities at the back of the book. Then ask him or her to reread the story. Praise any improvement.

Yes, I can.

These animals ate tall plants.

They had long necks.

11

These animals
could fly.

They had big wings.

hey had smooth flippers.

15

These animals were slow.

They had spiky armour.

17

These animals were fast.

They had strong legs.

19

I love that book.

Toys

Discussion Questions

1. What do the flying animals use to fly?

2. Why do you think some dinosaurs had armour?

3. Which animal would you like to meet? Why?

∿ Sight Words ∿

Learning sight words helps you read fluently. Practise these sight words from the book. Use them in sentences of your own.

these

that

can

were

they

you

had

I

✃ Rhyming Words ✃

Can you find the rhyming pairs?
Say them aloud.

book

ran

that

took

cat

can

Writing Practice

Read the words, and then trace them with your finger.

love

fast

slow

book

read

wings

❧ Silly Sentences ❧

Have fun filling in the gap in each
sentence. Use the ideas below
or make up your own.

These animals could ....

They had big ....